Best-
Cakes & Slices

Annabelle White

PENGUIN BOOKS

For their assistance with and contribution to this book, my thanks to
Kieran Scott (for the photographs), and Nicola Hudson (food assistant).
This book is dedicated to Lloyd Anderson for all his help and support.

PENGUIN BOOKS

Penguin Books (NZ) Ltd, cnr Airborne and Rosedale Roads, Albany,
Auckland 1310, New Zealand
Penguin Books Ltd, 27 Wrights Lane, London W8 5TZ, England
Penguin USA, 375 Hudson Street, New York, NY 10014, United States
Penguin Books Australia Ltd, 487 Maroondah Highway, Ringwood, Australia 3134
Penguin Books Canada Ltd, 10 Alcorn Avenue, Toronto, Ontario, Canada M4V 3B2
Penguin Books (South Africa) Pty Ltd, 5 Watkins Street, Denver Ext 4. 2094, South Africa
Penguin Books India (P) Ltd, 11, Community Centre, Panchsheel Park,
New Delhi 110 017, India

Penguin Books Ltd, Registered Offices: Harmondsworth, Middlesex, England

First published by Penguin Books (NZ) Ltd, 2000

1 3 5 7 9 10 8 6 4 2

Copyright © text and illustrations Annabelle White

Copyright © design Penguin Books (NZ) Ltd 2000
The right of Annabelle White to be identified as the author of this work in terms of
section 96 of the Copyright Act 1994 is hereby asserted.

Photography by Kieran Scott
Typesetting by Janine Brougham
Printed in Hong Kong by Condor Production Ltd
ISBN 014 029382 5

CONTENTS

INTRODUCTION **4**

Angel Food Cake with Lemon Zest topped with Berries **6**

Apple Shortcake **8**

Apricot Cinnamon Teacake **10**

Apricot Crumble Slice **12**

Aunty Alice's Tower Squares **14**

Bella's Super Simple Christmas Cake **16**

Berry & Almond Friands **18**

Caramel Slice **20**

Carrot & Walnut Cake **22**

Coconut Syrup Cake **24**

Date Cake **26**

Easy Gingerbread **28**

Ginger Crunch **30**

Graeme's Cherry Almond Cake **32**

Hedgehog Slice **34**

Lady Glenorchy's Super Simple Chocolate Cake **36**

Louise Cake **38**

Mini Coffee Cakes **40**

Muesli Slice **42**

One Pan Chocolate Cake with Ganache Icing **44**

Pandoro Chocolate Brownie **46**

Passionfruit Cheesecake Slice **48**

Pear & Ginger Upside Down Cake **50**

Peppermint Slice **52**

Raspberry Meringue Cake **54**

Rhubarb Sour Cream Cake **56**

Simply the Best Banana Cake **58**

Strawberry Swiss Roll **60**

Warm Toffee Macadamia Nut Cake **62**

Introduction

Baking cakes and slices brings back glorious childhood memories. Just think about visiting your grandparents and you can recall vivid images of fine china and cream cakes, scones, pikelets with home-made jam or luscious slices made for the occasion. Or perhaps, it's those journeys down hot and dusty roads to partake in welcoming lavish afternoon teas on family visits. Or even the daily return from school, to Mum and those unforgettably familiar sounds of a whistling kettle and cake tins being opened.

This is nurturing stuff and a source of great happiness. While demanding schedules prevent daily baking you may like to start a family tradition of a special baked item for the weekend – hoping some will last for lunch-boxes during the week. Baking is also a wonderful means to encourage a passion for cooking in young cooks. If they can master a cake or slice, they may be motivated further to help with dinner preparation.

This collection is full of easy-to-make, uncomplicated recipes that are simply superb. Not only will you find inspiration for a special morning or afternoon tea – you will also be inspired to create something fabulous for dessert. Either a decadent cream cake or a tray of mixed slices with coffee makes a grand finale to a dinner.

So enjoy this collection and use this book frequently. Let the sound of rattling cake tins begin!

- We used butter and fresh farm eggs for our recipes – search out the best raw ingredients and never keep ingredients for too long. For example, if a cake does not rise as you would expect buy some fresh baking powder to replace your old packet. Also don't be afraid to try new ingredients when baking traditional favourites – the addition of yoghurt or buttermilk, for example, produces a very moist cake.

- Cake tin sizes have been given as a guide only. Remember, if you use a larger cake tin the cooking time will be less. If you use a smaller tin, you need to allow for longer cooking time.

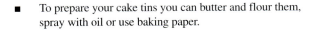

- To prepare your cake tins you can butter and flour them, spray with oil or use baking paper.

- Do not use fan bake when baking cakes, it tends to dry them out. We used regular bake in a Fisher & Paykel Astro double wall oven for all our baking – with very pleasing results.

Annabelle White

The sound of cream being whipped and the sight of brilliantly coloured fruit always generates a great deal of delight. This dessert cake looks very glamorous and difficult and yet it's super simple.

Angel Food Cake *with Lemon Zest topped with Berrie*

300 ml or 1 ¼ cups or 8 egg whites

1 ½ cups caster sugar

2 tbsp lemon zest

¼ tsp salt

1 ¼ tsp cream of tartar

1 cup plain flour, sifted

300 ml cream, whipped

1 punnet strawberries

1 punnet raspberries

6 strawberries, stalks on

12 fresh cherries

METHOD

Preheat the oven to 160°C. Beat the egg whites in a mixer until firm. Gradually add sugar, lemon zest, salt and cream of tartar. Sift flour onto egg whites and fold in carefully Pour into an oiled and papered 20 cm round tin or rin tin. The mixture will be above the rim. Bake for approximately one hour or until the top is lightly browned. Test with a skewer and ensure that it comes cleanly from the cake. Cool first, then remove from the tin. Decorate with unsweetened whipped cream and berries.

COOK'S TIP: Specialty cake shops sell angel food cake tins. These large ring tins are useful to have in your kitchen as they are perfect for all large cake mixtures. When testing this cake we found that unsweetened whipped cream worked well. Decorate with whipped cream, top with berries and serve immediately. Do not attempt to decorate and leave standing for a long period of time as this light cake with heavy fresh fruit topping is designed to be enjoyed straight away.

This is delicious frozen and reheated as needed. It's a real bonus for the home cook to find a recipe that so easily and successfully can be prepared ahead and re-created from the freezer!

Apple Shortcake

370 g butter

1½ cups caster sugar

4 eggs

3 cups plain flour

2 tsp cinnamon

500 g tin sliced pie apple

4 tbsp extra sugar

METHOD

Preheat oven to 180°C. Line a baking tray with baking paper. Cream butter and sugar and add eggs. Fold in flour and cinnamon. Place half mixture in prepared tin. Press down. Pat pie apple onto base. Sprinkle with 2 tbsp extra sugar. Place remaining batter on top. Sprinkle remaining 2 tbsp sugar on top. Bake at 180°C for approximately 45 minutes.

When this cake was tested at home some builders work
on a fence just outside the kitchen commented on the
delicious wafting aromas and quickly demolished sever
slices. The next day they appeared again at morning te
time and it seems that daily visits to check the stabilit
of the fence are now in order!

Apricot
Cinnamon Teacake

¾ cup prunes

¾ cup dried apricots

boiling water

2 cups flour

2 tsp baking powder

½ tsp salt

½ cup brown sugar

1 tbsp cinnamon

1 tbsp flour (extra)

200 g butter

170 g or ¾ cup sugar

2 eggs

¾ cup milk

1 tsp vanilla

6 tbsp melted butter

METHOD

Grease and flour a 22 cm tin. Soak fruit in boiling water for
five minutes; drain and halve. Sift flour, baking powd
and salt. In another bowl, mix brown sugar, cinnamon and
1 tbsp flour. Cream butter and sugar, add eggs and beat we
Add flour mixture alternately with milk and vanilla. Add frui
Put ⅓ batter into tin. Sprinkle with ⅓ brown sugar
mixture and 2 tbsp melted butter. Repeat two times. Place i
fridge overnight. Bake at 180°C for 55 minutes. Cool
tin on wire rack for 25 minutes prior to removing from tin.

A deliciously 'healthy' way to end a meal. All those rol
oats are great for the digestive system. Serve a slice w
custard or ice-cream and cream.

Apricot Crumble Slice

1 cup self-raising flour

1½ cups plain flour

1 cup brown sugar

1½ cups coconut

1 cup rolled oats

350 g melted butter

5 tbsp honey

1 cup sultanas

½ cup chopped
dried apricots

1 tsp cinnamon

2 x 425 g cans apricot halves,
drained

½ cup shredded coconut

METHOD

Preheat the oven to 180°C. Grease and prepare a 26 cm
loose-bottomed cake tin. Combine in a bowl all
ingredients except the last two. Press half the mixture
into the cake tin and spread the apricot halves (well drained
over the base. Crumble the remaining mix on top and press
down gently. Finish with the shredded coconut. Bake
at 180°C for 45 minutes.

COOK'S TIP: Serve warm, not hot. Ideally this should be made
the day ahead and then gently reheated as required.

Aunty Alice tells me her immediate family have been
demanding this slice in the tins for years. This is an
'I just have to have another little piece' number – you
will simply love it. A real family favourite!

Aunty Alice's Tower Squares

125 g butter

1 cup sugar

2 eggs

1 dessertspoon
golden syrup

1 cup sultanas

2 cups plain flour

2 tsp baking powder

ICING

2 cups icing sugar

25 g butter, softened

2 tbsp hot water

½ cup toasted
coconut threads

METHOD

Preheat oven to 160°C. Grease a 20 cm x 30 cm slice tin.
Cream butter and sugar until light and fluffy. Add egg
and beat in with golden syrup. Fold sultanas into 1 cup of th
flour to coat. Add to creamed mixture, plus remaining cup
flour and baking powder. Bake at 160°C for 30 minut
or until firm in centre. When cool, spread with icing
(mix together icing sugar, butter and hot water until smooth
and sprinkle with toasted shredded coconut.

This is a super recipe and you will love the results.
It makes a great Christmas present — for that
person who loves fruitcake and has a good supply
of socks! You can even make it on Christmas Eve
and it tastes great.

Bella's
Super Simple
Christmas Cake

1 kg dried fruit
(I use a mix of raisins,
currants and sultanas)

250 g chopped apricots

250 g butter

1 cup brown sugar

½ cup brandy or orange juice

½ cup cold tea or water

4 tsp finely grated
orange rind

2-3 tsp finely grated
lemon rind

1 tbsp treacle

5 large eggs, lightly beaten

2 cups high-grade flour

1 tsp baking powder

½ tsp baking soda

whole blanched almonds

extra brandy

METHOD

Line a deep 23 cm round or 20 cm square cake tin with
three layers of paper, bringing the paper 5 cm above the
edge of the cake tin. Combine all the dried fruits in
a large pot. Add the butter, sugar, brandy/orange juice and
cold tea/water. Stir over heat until butter is melted and sugar
is dissolved. Simmer, covered, 10 minutes. Cool to room
temperature. Stir in orange and lemon rind. Add
treacle and eggs. Sift and add dry ingredients. Mix in with
gentle folding movements. Spread mixture evenly
into the prepared tin and decorate the top with almonds.
Bake in a slow 150˚C oven for 2½-3 hours. When the
cake comes out of the oven, splash a little extra brandy over
the top. Cover hot cake with a few clean teatowels
and leave to cool in the pan, preferably overnight.

COOK'S TIP: We used Champion High Grade Flour for this fruitcake. The high grade helps prevent the fruit from sinking to the
bottom of the cake. Elsewhere in this book we used Champion
Standard Grade White Flour with great results.

Berry & Almond Friands

180 g butter, melted

1 cup ground almonds

5 egg whites

250 g or 2 cups icing sugar

½ cup plain flour

raspberries or blueberries

METHOD

Preheat the oven to 190°C. Grease 12 muffin pans. Place the melted butter, ground almonds, egg whites, icing sugar and flour in a bowl and mix thoroughly. Divide between the 12 pans and place three raspberries or blueberries in each muffin pan. Bake at 190°C for 25 minutes.

COOK'S TIP: These incredibly simple, delicious delights can be made to serve with coffee at the end of a special meal. You can vary the berries if desired — boysenberries or blackberries would work just as well.

Caramel Slice

Everyone loves this slice. It's so good, don't just serve with a cup of tea mid-afternoon — forget dessert an serve a slice to dinner guests with coffee. It is a class performer. At all times it's best eaten with tea, coffee o glass of milk. This is a very moreish version of the classic, as it has the addition of coconut in the base.

BASE

2½ cups self-raising flour

2 cups coconut

1 cup caster sugar

250 g butter, melted

CARAMEL

397 g can sweetened condensed milk

60 g butter

2 tbsp golden syrup

ICING

400 g dark chocolate

100 g butter

METHOD

Place all dry ingredients in a bowl. Add melted butter. Press firmly into a greased 20 cm x 30 cm sponge-roll tin. Bake at 180°C for 12 minutes or until lightly browned. Place all the caramel ingredients in a pan. Bring to the boil. Stir, simmering, for approximately four minutes. Sprea over base. Place in a 180°C oven for a further 10 minutes. Cool. For the icing, melt the chocolate and butter and spread over the caramel. Place in the fridge to se

This super-moist crowd pleaser is a delicious delight for afternoon tea or supper. It is so simple to make — and you can remind yourself that eating all those carrots is great for your eyesight!

Carrot & Walnut Cake

300 g or approx. 2½ cups plain flour

2 tsp baking soda

1 tsp salt

1 tsp mixed spice

1 tsp cinnamon

4 eggs, lightly beaten

165 g or approx. ⅔-¾ cup brown sugar

290 g or 1½ cups sugar

370 ml olive oil

200 g or approx 2 cups grated carrot

135 g crushed pineapple, drained

½ cup chopped walnuts

METHOD

Preheat the oven to 160°C. Mix the dry ingredients together. Slowly add the other ingredients in the order given. Pour into a greased 26 cm ring tin. Bake at 160°C for approximately 1½ hours or until a skewer comes out cleanly. Ice with lemon cream cheese icing (see page 58).

This makes a large café-style cake that would make a great dessert at a large luncheon. You could easily feed 15 people with this cake. Sensational!

Coconut Syrup Cake

250 g butter

450 g or 2¼ cups sugar

8 eggs

2 tsp lime zest

350 g or approx. 4½ cups coconut

320 g or 2½ cups self-raising flour

ORANGE WATER

250 g sugar

250 ml water

1 orange, quartered

TOPPING

160 g or ¾ cup brown sugar

250 ml cream

160 g or 2 cups coconut threads

METHOD

Preheat the oven to 150°C. Grease and line a 26 cm cake tin. Cream the butter and sugar and slowly add the eggs and lime zest. Fold in dry ingredients. Bake at 150°C for approximately two hours or until a skewer comes out cleanly when tested. Remove from oven. Using a skewer, poke about 12 holes in the top of the cake. Allow to cool.

While the cake is cooling heat the sugar, water and orange segments in a pan to make the orange water. Allow the mixture to infuse for as long as possible. Strain out the orange segments and pour the orange water over the cake.

For the topping, heat the brown sugar and cream in a pan and take off the heat when the sugar has dissolved, but prior to boiling. Add the coconut threads. Place on top of the cake and grill for a few minutes until lightly browned.

Date Cake

370 g dates

500 ml water

120 g butter

370 g or 1¾ cups brown sugar

370 g or 3 cups plain flour

2 tsp baking powder

4 eggs, lightly beaten

METHOD

Boil the dates, water and butter until you have achieved a jam consistency. Allow 10 minutes on a medium heat. Stir from time to time. Preheat the oven to 180˚C. Place the brown sugar, flour, baking powder and eggs in a bowl. Add the date mixture and mix to combine. Pour into a prepared square 20 cm cake tin. Bake at 180˚C for approximately 55 minutes or until a skewer comes out clean

COOK'S TIP: This cake makes a great addition to a lunchbox. Ever moist and delicious flavours always!

This can be sliced and buttered or eaten as is.

Easy
Gingerbread

200 g butter

¾ cup brown sugar

1 cup golden syrup

¾ cup milk

2 eggs

2 cups plain flour

1 tbsp ground ginger

1 tsp baking soda

1 tsp ground cinnamon

1 tsp mixed spice

2 tbsp chopped
crystallised ginger

METHOD

Place the butter, brown sugar, golden syrup and milk in a pan. Heat until the sugar dissolves. Do not boil. Remove from the heat and allow to cool. When cool, beat in eggs. Preheat the oven to 160°C. Sift all the dry ingredients into a bowl. Add the crystallised ginger. Make a well in the dry ingredients and add the liquid mixture. Stir until just combined. Pour into a greased loaf tin or 20 cm square tin. Bake at 160°C for 50-55 minutes.

COOK'S TIP: When it is warm from the oven this gingerbread makes a great base for an autumnal fruit compote and clotted cream dessert. Place a warm slice of gingerbread in a bowl, top with a ladle of apricot/pear/prune and apple compote and a dollop of cream. Sublime. Another great suggestion is to serve a slice of this gingerbread as the base for poached pears or tamarillos. Just top with custard!

We should eat more ginger. In former times, ginger was used as a cure-all for many medicinal problems. Just think, a slice of ginger crunch and a cup of tea could be a health treatment!

Ginger Crunch

190 g butter

½ cup sugar

2 cups flour

1½ tsp baking powder

1 tsp ground ginger

25 g or 3 tbsp crystallised ginger

GINGER ICING

100 g butter

2 cups icing sugar

2 tbsp golden syrup

3 tsp ground ginger

METHOD

Preheat the oven to 180°C. Cream the butter and sugar and then mix in all the dry ingredients. Press the mixture into a 20 cm x 30 cm slice tin. Bake at 180°C for 20 minutes. Ice with warm icing. Cut the slice before the base is completely cold.

ICING METHOD

Place all the icing ingredients in a saucepan and heat until combined. Pour over cooled biscuit base.

My cousin and great friend Graeme Moran loves to recount the time he invited the late Earl Spencer and Countess Raine Spencer to tea in his modest home in London. He dusted off the silver tea service and served this cake — it went down a treat. As the father to the late Princess of Wales, the Earl Spencer's enthusiasm for the cake was almost akin to a 'cake by Royal Appointment' for Graeme.

Graeme's Cherry Almond Cake

250 g or 2 cups self-raising flour

150 g ground almonds

350 g glacé cherries

250 g butter

250 g or 1¼ cups sugar

5 eggs

½ cup flaked almonds

METHOD

Preheat the oven to 160°C. Grease and line a 20 cm cake tin with baking paper. Blend the flour and ground almonds together in a bowl. Fold cherries into flour/almond mixture and coat thoroughly. Cream butter and sugar and add eggs. Beat well. Fold in flour/cherry mixture. Spoon into the prepared cake tin. Sprinkle over with the flaked almonds. Bake at 160°C for 1½ hours or until a skewer comes out cleanly.

COOK'S TIP: By coating the cherries in the almond/flour mixture first they are less likely to sink to the bottom of the cake!

This is especially designed for all the serious chocolate lovers — intensely chocolate, full of crunch and with the contrasting flavours of dried apricots and sultanas — sublime!

Hedgehog Slice

350 g dark chocolate pieces

175 g butter

1½ cups chopped wine biscuits

1 cup sultanas

½ cup dried apricots, sliced

METHOD

Melt chocolate and butter. Fold in biscuits, sultanas and apricots. Generously line a loaf pan with plastic wrap. Pour the mix into loaf tin. Place in the fridge to set.

COOK'S TIP: Nuts can be added to this mix if desired. For extra-quick results, whiz your biscuits in the food processor. The plastic wrap makes it easy to lift out of the pan and slice. Run your knife under the hot water tap for a few seconds before slicing this chocolate extravaganza.

A fellow foodie and friend, Deb Alley of Queenstown, is such an elegant hostess and cook that friends have dubbed her 'Lady Glenorchy'. This is the easiest and most delicious cake — better still, it improves with keeping.

Lady Glenorchy's
Super Simple
Chocolate Cake

2 cups white sugar

2 eggs

1 cup plain yoghurt

¾ cup cocoa

200 g melted butter

2 tsp baking soda

1½ tsp vanilla

¼ tsp salt

3 cups self-raising flour

1 cup boiling strong coffee

METHOD

Place all ingredients in the order given into a food processor bowl. Process for one minute. Pour mixture into a greased deep 23 x 33 cm square or similar-sized round cake tin. Bake at 160°C for approximately 1¼ hours. Cool in tin before removing and ice with your favourite chocolate icing.

COOK'S TIP: Slice this un-iced cake in half and freeze one part, keeping the other for immediate use. Later you can use the cake for a sensational trifle. Try blackberries and raspberries, kirsch or crème de cassis, chocolate cake, custard and cream for the most amazing dessert!

Louise Cake

No cake or slice collection would be complete without a traditional Louise Cake. We used strawberry jam rather than the traditional raspberry — but there are no hard and fast rules about which jam to select. Plum would be delicious and so would apricot. I'm sure Louise wouldn't mind at all!

150 g butter

¾ cup sugar

4 egg yolks

2½ cups plain flour

2 tsp baking powder

375 g strawberry jam

4 egg whites

½ cup sugar

1½ cups desiccated coconut

¼ cup coconut threads

METHOD

Preheat the oven to 180°C. Grease a 20 cm x 30 cm slice tin. Cream the butter and sugar. Add egg yolks. Fold in the flour and the baking powder. Press into the slice tin. Spread over the jam. Whisk the egg whites and sugar in a clean bowl until firm. Fold in desiccated coconut. Spread carefully over the jam. Sprinkle with coconut threads. Bake at 180°C for 30 minutes.

COOK'S TIP: Remember always to buy fresh coconut as you need it for your baking. You get far better results if you buy small amounts rather than keeping a large amount in your pantry. This slice is so delicious you can cut it into small slices and serve it with coffee instead of a dessert. Perhaps combine it with servings of the Pandoro Brownie so there is a selection — everyone will be impressed with your efforts in the kitchen.

It can be fun to make individual cakes to serve a crowd rather than messing about slicing each portion. This mixture makes 18 muffin-sized coffee cakes.

Mini Coffee Cakes

150 g butter

1 cup milk

4 eggs

1 cup caster sugar

2 cups self-raising flour

3 tbsp instant coffee

3 tsp hot water

COFFEE ICING

2 cups icing sugar

25 g soft butter

3 tsp instant coffee

1 tbsp boiling water

METHOD

Preheat the oven to 180°C. Spray 12 muffin-sized tins.
Heat the butter and milk until the butter has melted. Beat the eggs until thick and slowly add the sugar. Fold in the cooled milk and butter, and dry ingredients. Dissolve the instant coffee in the hot water and fold this into the mixture. Bake at 180°C for approximately 25 minutes. Ice with coffee icing.

ICING METHOD

Combine together in a large bowl and blend well until you have the desired consistency.

COOK'S TIP: With all my baking I use eggs at room temperature, not straight from the fridge — particularly where the eggs and sugar are beaten together to create super-light cakes. The extra volume created by room-temperature eggs versus cold eggs greatly enhances these cakes.

Muesli Slice

250g butter

½ cup caster sugar

3 tbsp honey

1 tbsp peanut butter

2½ cups rolled oats

¾ cup coconut

70g flaked almonds

¼ tsp cinnamon

¼ tsp mixed spice

1 tbsp sunflower seeds

1 tbsp pumpkin seeds

1 cup dried apricots, chopped

1 cup sultanas

¾ cup chopped dates

¼ cup shredded coconut

METHOD

Preheat the oven to 160°C. Grease a 20 x 30cm Swiss-roll tin Heat the butter, sugar, honey and peanut butter in a saucepan. Place all the other ingredients in a large bowl. Add the wet mixture to the dry mix. Stir to combine. Press into the tin and bake at 160°C for approximately 40 minutes or until golden in colour.

This is the most amazing cake — it keeps beautifully and the results are quite stunning!

One Pan Chocolate Cake

With Ganache Icin

115 g or ½ cup butter

125 g dark chocolate

1 cup sugar

1 tsp vanilla

1¾ cups buttermilk

3 eggs

1¾ cups plain flour

1 tsp baking soda

½ tsp salt

½ tsp baking powder

ICING

50 g butter

50 g dark chocolate

METHOD

Heat oven to 180°C. Grease a 22 cm tin. Dust with cocoa. Heat butter and chocolate in saucepan. When melted, add sugar and vanilla. Whisk in buttermilk and eggs. Add dry ingredients and whisk until smooth. Pour batter into tin. Bake for 40 minutes or until skewer comes out clean. Turn out onto wire rack to cool. Heat 50 g butter and 50 g dark chocolate together in microwave, stirring every 30 seconds until melted. Pour over cooled cake.

COOK'S TIP: We chose Tararua buttermilk for this cake with delicious results. Buttermilk is a versatile ingredient to have in the fridge — it adds tang and moistness to cakes, muffins, scones and pancakes, and best of all the shelf life is quite incredible — it will be fine in the fridge unopened for weeks.

Pandoro, a well-known name associated with great breads and baking, makes a divine chocolate brownie. In a word, it's a living legend. Everyone loves this delicious chocolate masterpiece. Thank you to the team at Pandoro for parting with this recipe — it is a real gem!

Pandoro Chocolate Brownie

100 g cocoa

200 g butter, melted

400 g or 2 cups caster sugar

4 eggs

1 tsp vanilla

90 g flour or just under ¾ cups

1 tsp baking powder

200 g chocolate chips

METHOD

Sift cocoa into a large mixing bowl. Add melted butter, sugar eggs and vanilla. Mix to a smooth paste. Sift in flour and baking powder, and then add chocolate chips. Pour mixture into a 20 cm x 30 cm Swiss-roll tin. Bake in a preheated oven at 150°C for 65 minutes.

COOK'S TIP: Mixture should feel a little undercooked. Slice when completely cooled. Do not be alarmed at the amount of sugar in this recipe — this is the correct amount and not a misprint.

Passionfruit Cheesecake Slice

BASE

1 cup flour

½ cup sugar

125 g butter, softened

1 egg yolk

TOPPING

500 g cream cheese

200 g or 1 cup sugar

7 tbsp flour

3 tbsp cream

2 eggs and 1 yolk

½ cup passionfruit pulp

METHOD

Mix all base ingredients in cake mixer. Press into greased high-sided 20 cm x 30 cm Swiss-roll tin.

TOPPING METHOD

Place all ingredients in cake mixer. Beat until combined and smooth. Pour over the base. Bake in preheated oven 180°C for 40 minutes.

COOK'S TIP: Serve for dessert with extra passionfruit pulp and cream. This cheesecake freezes well.

This cake would make a delicious pudding with custard and cream.

Pear & Ginger Upside-Down Cake

150 g butter

½ cup brown sugar

1 egg

2 tbsp golden syrup

1½ cups plain flour

¼ tsp cinnamon

1 tsp ground ginger

1½ tsp baking powder

½ tsp ground cloves

¼ tsp salt

1 tsp baking soda

½ cup hot water

¼ cup crystallised ginger, finely chopped

¾ cup chopped pears, fresh or canned

METHOD

Make topping first, then the cake. For the cake, cream butter and sugar. Add egg. Mix well and add syrup. Blend all together. Sift together dry ingredients. Fold in half the creamed butter mixture, then half the hot water. Repeat Finally, add ginger and pears. Bake at 180°C for 1½ hours or until skewer comes out clean.

TOPPING

100 g butter

¾ cup brown sugar

3 pears, peeled, halved and cored (or use 410 g tin)

TOPPING METHOD

Melt butter and add brown sugar. Place pears face down in 20 cm prepared tin. Pour sugar mixture over the pear and place cake batter on top.

Peppermint and chocolate is a simply irresistible combination. That rich, creamy chocolate contrasted with the refreshing zing of peppermint — every mouthful is memorable.

Peppermint Slice

BASE

1½ cups self-raising flour

½ cup cocoa

1 cup desiccated coconut

¾ cup sugar

150 g butter, melted

1 egg

PEPPERMINT FILLING

3 cups icing sugar

50 g butter, softened

2 tsp peppermint essence

1 tbsp melted Kremelta

CHOCOLATE ICING

400 g chocolate

100 g butter

METHOD

Preheat the oven to 180°C. Prepare a 20 cm x 30 cm Swiss-roll tin by spraying with oil or greasing well with butter. Place the flour, cocoa, coconut and sugar in a bowl and add melted butter and egg. Mix well and press into the baking tin. Bake at 180°C for 15 minutes.

TO MAKE THE PEPPERMINT FILLING:

Combine all the ingredients and blend well. Spread over the cooked and cooled base. Place in the fridge for 30 minutes to set, then ice with chocolate icing.

TO MAKE THE CHOCOLATE ICING:

Heat the butter and chocolate together in a small saucepan microwave and smear gently over the peppermint topping.

Blosssoms Café in West Auckland serves up such great baking that people travel from far and wide to sample their delights. One absolute show-stopper is Kylie's Raspberry Meringue Cake. One mouthful and you really think you have died and gone to heaven. Serve this cake on Valentine's Day!

Raspberry Meringue Cake

CAKE BASE

90 g butter

⅓ cup caster sugar

5 egg yolks

1 tsp vanilla

¼ cup cream

⅓ cup plain flour

2 tbsp cornflour

2 tsp baking powder

MERINGUE TOPPING

5 egg whites

1 cup caster sugar

1 tsp vanilla

RASPBERRY FILLING

2 punnets raspberries

1 cup cream

1 tbsp icing sugar

½ tsp vanilla

METHOD FOR CAKE

Preheat oven to 170°C. Spray and line two 23 cm cake tins with baking paper. Cream butter and sugar. Beat yolks, and add to creamed mixture, mixing well. Add vanilla and cream and mix through. Sift flour, cornflour and baking powder over top, then fold through cake mixture. Divide mixture into both tins.

TO MAKE MERINGUE

Beat egg whites until stiff, gradually add sugar and beat until soft peaks form. Fold through vanilla. Spread meringue over cake. Bake in preheated oven for about 35 minutes, or until skewer comes out clean. Leave to cool in the tins.

TO MAKE FILLING

Whip cream until stiff, then add icing sugar and vanilla. Fold through half the berries. Lightly crush the other half and fold through.

TO ASSEMBLE

Turn one cake out onto the platter meringue side down. Remove baking paper and cover with the raspberry cream. Place other layer on top meringue side up. Sift some extra icing sugar on top. Take cake out of fridge an hour before serving.

Sour cream adds a whole new dimension to a home-baked cake. Moist and with the lightest texture, you will be delighted with the results. Use this basic sour cream cake mix to make your favourite citrus sour cream cake. This recipe is an all-time favourite!

Rhubarb
Sour Cream Cake

250 g softened butter

2 cups sugar

6 lightly beaten large eggs

2 cups flour

2 tsp baking powder

1 tsp cinnamon

1 cup light sour cream

540 g tin rhubarb, well drained

GLAZE

Juice of 1 orange and ¼ cup sugar

METHOD

Cream butter and sugar until light and fluffy. Add eggs and blend well. Fold in flour, baking powder and cinnamon alternately with sour cream and rhubarb. Mix gently until smooth and pour into a well-greased 24-26 cm spring-bottom round tin. Bake at 160°C for 60-70 minutes or until skewer comes out clean when tested. After baking, leave cake in tin for a few minutes, then pour on glaze. Leave for another few minutes and then remove from pan.

COOK'S TIP: If you have a healthy supply of rhubarb in the garden, just poach some slices of rhubarb in a boiling sugar syrup for a few minutes only. Drain well and use as you would the canned variety. You can substitute the orange and sugar glaze for a little of the rhubarb liquid or juice if desired — just be careful not to use too much or the cake will be soggy.

Simply The Best Banana Cake

Another recipe from Deb — when she was running her b[?] café in Queenstown this recipe was a hit with all the regulars. Banana cake appeals to everyone and is the perfect means of using overripe bananas.

2½ cups self-raising flour

1 tsp baking soda

1 cup caster sugar

4 eggs

2½ cups mashed bananas (about 4 bananas)

1 cup oil

CREAM CHEESE ICING

100 g cream cheese

60 g butter, softened

juice of ½ lemon

2 tsp lemon zest

METHOD

Sift the flour and soda into a bowl. Make a well and stir in th[?] sugar, eggs, banana and oil. Mix gently to a smooth batter. Pour into a greased and baking paper lined 20 cm round tin. Bake at 160˚C for approximately 1½ hours[?] Ice with lemon cream cheese icing.

ICING METHOD

Blend together all ingredients vigorously (I use my food processor). Add more lemon juice if you prefer a sharper, more distinctively lemon flavour.

COOK'S TIP: We used a 20 cm cake tin to produce an impressively high banana cake. If you prefer to use a larger tin, adjust your cooking times — it will take less time to cook.

This is a very elegant addition to a special afternoon tea or sweet finale for a glamorous lunch. Everyone loves sponge, cream and strawberries!

Strawberry Swiss Roll

3 eggs

5 tbsp caster sugar

4 tbsp plain flour

4 tbsp cornflour

300 ml whipped cream

1 large punnet or 225 g strawberries

METHOD

Preheat oven to 220°C. Line a 33 x 23 cm baking tray with baking paper. Whisk eggs and sugar until very thick. When you lift the beaters it should leave a ribbon design on the mix. Sift flour and cornflour over egg mixture and fold i with a large metal spoon. Spread evenly onto baking tray. Bake near the top of the oven for 10-12 minutes or until springy to touch. Spread a clean teatowel on a work surface. Turn sponge onto it and allow to cool. Remov paper. When cool, spread whipped cream over spong and place strawberries on top. Roll from short end, lifting teatowel carefully.

COOK'S TIP: This log can be assembled four hours prior to serving.

Another Blosssom's delight — a sensational,
moist nut cake — in a word, yum!
Thank you to Pete and Kylie Adams.

Warm Toffee Macadamia Nut Cake

NUTS

80 g chopped macadamia nuts

80 g chopped Brazil nuts

50 g coconut

additional nuts for the topping

TOFFEE

120 g butter

160 g cream

300 g or 1½ cups brown sugar

CAKE

220 g butter, softened

360 g approximately
1¾ cups sugar

6 large eggs

2 tsp vanilla

220 ml milk

320 g approximately
2½ cups self-raising flour

2 tsp cinnamon

METHOD

Toast nuts and coconut in a 160°C oven and spread in greased and paper-lined 22cm tin. Place the toffee ingredients into a pot and heat toffee mixture over low heat until smooth. Pour over nut mixture. Cream butter and sugar until light and fluffy. Add eggs one at a time and beat well after each addition. Add vanilla and mix well. Fold in milk with flour and cinnamon. Spoon over nut mixture. Bake at 160°C for 1 hour 55 minutes. Serve warm with thick cream or vanilla custard.

COOK'S TIP: This cake looks even more dramatic with the addition of extra nuts placed on top after baking and prior to serving.